To my friend Kaylee —

Happy Birthday!

Happy Baking!

♡ Melanie

QUICK
BREADS

QUICK BREADS

65 recipes for
bakers in a hurry

by Beatrice A. Ojakangas

Illustrations by Sally Sturman

Clarkson Potter/Publishers
New York

Published by Clarkson N. Potter, Inc., 201 East 50th Street, New
York, New York 10022. Member of the Crown Publishing Group.

CLARKSON POTTER, POTTER and colophon are trademarks of
Clarkson N. Potter, Inc.

Manufactured in the United States of America

Library of Congress Cataloging-in-Publication Data
Ojakangas, Beatrice A.
Quick breads: 65 recipes for bakers in a hurry/
by Beatrice A. Ojakangas. — 1st ed.
Includes index.
1. Bread. I. Title.
TX769.O386   1990
641.8'15—dc20   90-7433
ISBN 0-517-58013-6

Book design by Jan Melchior

10   9   8   7   6   5   4   3

CONTENTS

INTRODUCTION

Quick, fast, and served hot—for all those modern terms, quick breads are descendants of crude hearth cakes of primitive times. The Scottish poet Robert Burns wrote about "bannocks o' barley," a non-yeasted barley cake cooked over a fire. England's King Alfred is credited with having invented "quick cakes" by accident. He forgot to watch the pot of porridge as he sat in his hut, and discovered that it cooked into a bread. The American Indians taught the early colonists to bake cornmeal over a fire into hot cakes. It was a matter of history and inventiveness of cooks, as corn sticks and corn breads of many kinds were developed in different regions of our country.

Quick breads, as opposed to not-so-quick yeast breads, are loaves that require no kneading or rising. Their preparation goes quickly: many of them can be assembled in 10 to 15 minutes. What a boon to the busy cook! Though most quick breads taste great fresh and hot from the oven, many of them are even better the next day, and can be toasted to further concentrate and develop their flavor.

If I plan to have a quick bread to serve with a meal for company, I often assemble the ingredients ahead of time, to avoid last-minute "mess." Mix the dry ingredients in one bowl and the liquids in another so that they can be combined at the last minute. Then they can be stirred together to pop into the oven and be served piping hot minutes later.

Except for a few quick sticks and rolls, I've concentrated on quick loaves and coffee cakes that are versatile enough to be enjoyed at any time of day. Many of them are sufficiently festive to serve for special holiday meals. They're packed with good things like fruits, nuts, whole grains, seeds, spices, and even vegetables like carrots and zucchini, to make them quietly nourishing.

Tea breads in this collection, such as Golden Tangerine Nut Bread, Sour Cream Orange Filbert Bread, and Pistachio Nut Loaves, are light in color, crumb, and flavor and make a delightful snack with hot or iced tea or coffee, or a glass of milk. I like to add slices of lightly buttered tea breads to a cookie tray during the holidays.

Fruit and nut breads are dark and richly flavored. Old-time American favorites, like a loaf of Cheddar Date Nut, Fruited Apple, or Granola Chocolate Cherry, are great for holiday entertaining and gifts. Add a few thick slices to the bread basket for lunch or supper to delight your family or guests.

Savory quick breads are those speedy loaves that cooks around the world have relied on for generations. Some are rustic loaves with little or no sweetening, which rely on whole grains, spices, seeds, and herbs for flavoring, such as Herbed Irish Soda Bread, Finnish Barley Bread, and Australian Damper. All of the brown breads are low in fat but are remarkably rich-tasting, wonderful, close-textured breads that keep well and make great breakfast toast.

Quick sticks and rolls are little breads that are neither muffins nor scones nor biscuits, but are quick versions of some favorite yeast-raised breads. Cinnamon Raisin Rolls, Cardamom Buns, and Cheese Croissants are mixed, shaped, and baked with no waiting around for rising. Fanciful variations of early American classics are crispy Corn Puffs and two "new" corn sticks.

Old-fashioned coffee cakes are cakes for breakfast, brunch, or evening "after the meeting" snacking. Some are baked in fancy tube molds, such as Sour Cream Cinnamon Coffee Cake, while others are dessertlike, such as the Walnut Pear and Apple Pie coffee cakes. Most are best warm from the oven, but can be reheated in the microwave if made ahead and frozen.

Quick holiday breads are those breads with flavors that signify something special: cardamom, almonds, and fruits in a quick version of Norwegian Julekage; the perfume of lemon and anise in Italian Panettone; raisins in Quick Kugelhof; and raisins, orange peel, and a dash of rum in a quick version of classic Stollen.

Spreadable spreads are butters and cream cheese spreads that you can whip up and keep in a covered container in the refrigerator to further enhance the flavors of quick breads. Whipped butters and tasty cheese spreads can turn a savory bread into a first course.

In this book you will find well-tested, tried-and-true old basic favorites as well as some new and innovative ideas. I hope it will inspire you to grab an apron and head into the kitchen!

ABOUT INGREDIENTS
Flour

Flours differ in their protein content and you should check the information on the nutritional label of the sack. Quick breads, along with cakes, cookies, and pastries, turn out the best with all-purpose flour that contains 11 to 12 grams of protein per cup. This is the flour I used for testing the recipes in this book. (For yeast breads, I purchase all-purpose or bread flour that has 13 to 14 grams of protein per cup, which has the gluten necessary for yeast-raised breads.)

"Self-rising flour" is an all-purpose flour with leavening and salt added to it, and is popular in the South, especially for making biscuits. You cannot substitute self-rising flour for all-purpose flour without making adjustments in the leavening and salt in the recipe.

Baking powder

Of course, the freshest of ingredients will perform the best and taste the best. If you don't do a lot of baking, be sure to check the date on your baking powder can. While salt will not lose its saltiness, nor baking soda its properties, old baking powder does lose its strength. There should be a date stamped on the container somewhere, and if that date is past, discard the can and get a new one!

Eggs

All the recipes in this book were tested with "large" eggs. One large egg measures ¼ cup or 2 ounces. If necessary, you can substitute smaller or larger eggs, but you will have to measure them. To do this, beat the egg slightly to mix the yolk with the white, then measure. Usually, a little extra egg will not harm the recipe. Too little egg might make a mixture that is dry.

Spices

Check the age of the spices on your shelf, too. While old spices probably will not harm you, they often have lost their flavor. As a rule of thumb, your spices should be replaced every 6 months to a year. This will vary, of course, depending on where you keep them. Spices keep their aroma longer if they are kept in tightly closed containers, away from heat and sun.

Buttermilk

Buttermilk is an oft-used ingredient in quick breads. Even though buttermilk has a longer shelf life than milk, you might still have trouble using it up if you aren't a buttermilk lover. You can substitute fresh milk by adding 2 teaspoons of fresh lemon juice or white vinegar per cup of milk, and allowing the mixture to stand for 5 minutes to sour. Powdered buttermilk is another option; just follow the directions on the package.

Butter, margarine, and oil

Even though all of the recipes in this book were tested with and call for lightly salted butter, you can substitute unsalted butter, margarine, or shortening. Just be sure that the margarine you substitute has the same number of calories per tablespoon as butter. "Light" margarine will not give the same results as butter. Margarines that always stay soft may not give satisfactory results. Use a high-quality, firm margarine that has an acceptable taste. Margarine will never give the same flavor as butter will to a product. Oil cannot be substituted for butter, margarine, or solid shortening, as the liquid balance may be thrown off. It is safest to use oil only where oil is called for in a recipe.

Molasses, syrup, honey, and sugar

Generally, you cannot substitute molasses, syrup, or honey for sugar with the same results unless the amount is very small—one tablespoon or less. You can, however, safely substitute light molasses for dark and vice versa. Usually, you can interchange molasses, syrup, and honey, but expect characteristic flavors.

BAKING TIPS

Grinding, pulverizing, and crushing

These three terms all mean the same thing, and I use them interchangeably. You can accomplish this with a knife, by hand, with a mortar and pestle, or with a blender, food mill, coffee grinder, meat grinder, or food processor—each with somewhat different results. When it is important, a recipe will specify the preferred method.

Mixing quick bread doughs

You can use an electric mixer for creaming shortening, sugar, and eggs. In all recipes where "creaming" is called for, this is the easiest tool to use. However, when adding dry ingredients and liquid ingredients it is best to use a wooden spoon, to avoid overmixing. When quick bread batter or dough is overmixed, the finished product may have large holes and "tunnels" and the top of the bread will have an exaggerated "hump."

Pans

Quick breads can be baked in standard 9½ x 5½-inch (large), 8½ x 4½-inch (medium), or 5¾ x 3½-inch (small) loaf pans. They are interchangeable; however, the pans indicated with the recipe are the pans I used for testing, which will give you some idea of the volume of batter to expect.

Fancy tube pans, whimsically shaped molds, brioche pans, steamed-pudding molds, tin cans, and coffee cans can all be used for baking loaf breads. The batter should fill the pan two-thirds full for the best-shaped loaf. If the pan is overfilled, the bread will spill over the top and the texture will be coarse and porous. Bread baked in a pan that is too large will not brown on top and will be too dark on the bottom.

Baking

Let ovens preheat a full 15 minutes before baking loaf breads. The oven racks should be set as near the center of the oven as possible, unless a recipe directs otherwise.

If you bake several loaves at once, stagger the pans so that the heat will circulate as evenly as possible. Never let pans touch each other or the oven walls.

Testing for doneness

The breads in this book have been tested at the oven temperature listed in the recipe. Ovens need to be checked for accuracy. If your breads brown before the centers are done, the oven may be running too hot. If your breads are not done in the time specified, it may be too low. The best check is a mercury oven thermometer hung in the center of the oven from an oven rack.

Check bread after the minimum baking time, then bake longer if needed. To test for doneness, the most reliable method is to insert a wooden skewer into the center of the bread. If the skewer comes out clean and dry, the bread is cooked through. At this point, the edges of the bread will usually have pulled away from the sides of the pan. Breads that have little or no sugar in the recipe (such as a soda bread) will not brown much during baking, so you cannot judge doneness by browning. A crack down the center is characteristic of quick breads and cannot be prevented.

Serving breads

To slice quick bread loaves more easily, use a hot serrated bread knife (run quickly under hot water, then wipe dry). When slicing, use only the weight of the knife in a sawing motion. Most nut breads are delicious when toasted under the broiler.

Storing breads

If you do not plan to serve the bread immediately, wrap it as soon as it is cooled, label, and freeze. Nut breads can be sliced while still slightly frozen; serve as many slices as you need, then return the remainder of the loaf to the freezer.

TEA BREADS

⤸

Golden Tangerine Nut Bread

Poppy Seed Nut Bread

Coconut Strawberry Bread

Orange Pecan Bread

Sour Cream Orange Filbert Bread

Pumpkin Pecan Tea Bread

Cranberry Raisin Bread

Black Walnut Tea Bread

Cinnamon Pear Tea Bread

Lemon-Glazed Cardamom Pear Tea Bread

Cheddar Apple Bread

Zucchini Walnut Bread

Date Nut Cranberry Bread

Prune Walnut Bread

Pistachio Nut Bread

Golden Tangerine Nut Bread

A glaze made with fresh tangerine juice gives this bread moistness and flavor. The texture is cakelike and the flavor so wonderful that you may never find out that it keeps well, too!

½ cup (1 stick) butter, at room temperature

¾ cup sugar

2 eggs, at room temperature

1 tablespoon grated tangerine rind

1¼ cups all-purpose flour

1½ teaspoons baking powder

¼ teaspoon salt

½ cup coarsely chopped walnuts

1 tablespoon all-purpose flour

½ cup milk

GLAZE

3 tablespoons freshly squeezed tangerine juice

3 tablespoons sugar

Preheat the oven to 350° F. Grease and lightly flour one 8½ x 4½-inch loaf pan or two 5¾ x 3½-inch loaf pans.

In a large mixing bowl, cream the butter and ¾ cup of sugar together until blended. Add the eggs and beat until fluffy and light. Add the tangerine rind. In another bowl, stir the 1¼ cups of flour and the baking powder and salt together until blended.

Toss the walnuts with the 1 tablespoon of flour until all the pieces are lightly coated. Blend the flour mixture into the creamed mixture alternately with the milk. Fold the walnuts into the batter until blended. Turn into the prepared pans or pan. Bake 35 to 45 minutes for small loaves, 55 to 60 minutes for the medium loaf, or until they test done.

Meanwhile, combine the juice and sugar in a small pan to make the glaze. Heat just until the sugar is dissolved. Poke the hot loaves with a skewer or toothpick in several places and pour the syrup over them. Cool in the pan for 10 minutes, then remove and finish cooling on a rack.

Makes one medium or two small loaves

Poppy Seed
Nut Bread

❧

On sunny summer afternoons, I'll serve slices of this bread with Apricot Cream Cheese Spread (page 118) and fresh iced herb tea. To make a fresh herb tea, I cut a good-size bunch of lemon balm or spearmint from the garden and pack it into a large mixing bowl along with a few bags of raspberry and orange herbal tea; then I pour boiling water over it all and let it steep a half hour or so. When it is cool, I pour it over ice cubes and sweeten with a bit of honey.

---

5 tablespoons butter, at room
   temperature

1 cup sugar

2 eggs

2 cups all-purpose flour

2 teaspoons baking powder

½ teaspoon salt

¼ teaspoon freshly grated
   nutmeg

1 cup milk

⅓ cup poppy seeds

½ cup chopped walnuts or
   pecans

½ cup golden raisins

Preheat the oven to 350° F. Grease and flour a 9½ x 5½-inch loaf pan or three 5¾ x 3½-inch loaf pans.

In a large bowl, cream the butter and sugar until blended. Beat in the eggs, one at a time, until light. In another bowl, stir the flour, baking powder, salt, and nutmeg together until blended. Add the flour mixture alternately with the milk to the creamed mixture; blend well. Stir in the poppy seeds, nuts, and raisins.

Turn the batter into the prepared pan or pans. Bake 40 to 45 minutes for small loaves or 1 hour and 15 minutes for a large loaf, or until they test done. Remove from the pan and cool on a rack.

Makes one large or three small loaves

Coconut
Strawberry Bread

❦

Moist, sweet, and tart, this
bread is perfect with a luncheon salad.

2 eggs	½ teaspoon baking soda
½ cup vegetable oil	½ teaspoon freshly ground
¾ cup sugar	nutmeg
1½ cups sliced strawberries	½ teaspoon salt
2 cups all-purpose flour	1 cup shredded, sweetened
½ teaspoon ground cinnamon	coconut
1 teaspoon baking powder	¾ cup chopped pecans

Preheat the oven to 350° F. Grease and flour one 9½ x 5½-inch loaf pan or three 5¾ x 3½-inch loaf pans.

In a large bowl, beat the eggs until fluffy; add the oil and sugar and continue beating until light. Mix in the berries. In another bowl, combine the remaining ingredients. Add to the strawberry mixture, blending just until the flour is moistened; do not overmix. Spoon into the prepared pan or pans. Bake 50 to 60 minutes for the large loaf, 45 to 55 minutes for the small loaves, or until they test done. Cool in the pan for 5 minutes; loosen and turn out onto a rack to cool completely.

Makes one large or three small loaves

Orange
Pecan Bread

So delicious and so very quick! The aroma of orange peel wafts out of this bread when it's hot. To fit into a special diet, substitute 2 egg whites for the whole egg and use skim milk instead of whole milk.

¾ cup sugar

¼ cup vegetable oil

1 egg

1¼ cups milk

1 teaspoon salt

2 cups all-purpose flour

½ cup whole-wheat flour

1 tablespoon baking powder

3 tablespoons grated orange peel

1 cup chopped pecans

Preheat the oven to 350° F. Grease one 9½ x 5½-inch loaf pan or two 8½ x 4½-inch loaf pans.

Measure all of the ingredients into a large mixing bowl. Beat for 30 seconds. Pour into the pan or pans. Bake 55 to 65 minutes for the large loaf or 55 to 60 minutes for the two medium loaves, or until they test done. Cool in the pan for 5 minutes, then remove from the pan and finish cooling on a rack. Cool completely before slicing.

Makes one large or two medium loaves

Sour Cream Orange Filbert Bread

Toasting the nuts intensifies their flavor. Spread them on a baking sheet in a single layer and place in a 350° F. oven for 5 minutes. Stir once, or until the nuts are toasted; cool. The skins will be loose, so rub the nuts in a terry towel to remove most of them. Not all of the skins will come off, but that's okay; they will add a nice brown fleck to the bread.

2 tablespoons freshly grated orange rind

2 tablespoons (1/4 stick) butter, melted

1/4 teaspoon salt

1/2 cup sugar

2 eggs

2 cups all-purpose flour

2 teaspoons baking powder

1 teaspoon baking soda

1 1/2 cups sour cream

1 cup chopped, toasted filberts or pecans

Preheat the oven to 350° F. Grease one 9 1/2 x 5 1/2-inch loaf pan or three 5 3/4 x 3 1/2-inch loaf pans.

In a large bowl, cream together the orange rind, butter, salt, and sugar until blended. Add the eggs and beat until light. In another bowl, stir together the flour, baking powder, and soda.

Blend the dry ingredients into the creamed mixture alternately with the sour cream; mix just until blended. Stir in the nuts.

Spoon the mixture into the prepared pan or pans. Bake 50 to 60 minutes for the large loaf or 35 to 45 minutes for the smaller loaves, or until they test done.

Remove from the oven and cool for 5 minutes in the pan, then turn out onto a rack to finish cooling.

Makes one large or three small loaves

Pumpkin Pecan Tea Bread

❧

I've always loved the taste of pumpkin. This bread has a nice, even texture and is moist and spicy. If you don't have pumpkin-pie spice, you can use a combination of 2 teaspoons cinnamon, ½ teaspoon nutmeg, and ¼ teaspoon each of ground ginger and ground cloves.

⅔ cup (1⅓ sticks) butter, at room temperature

1¾ cups sugar

4 eggs

2 cups (one 15- to 16-ounce can) cooked pumpkin puree

⅔ cup milk

3½ cups all-purpose flour

1 tablespoon pumpkin-pie spice

3 teaspoons baking powder

½ teaspoon baking soda

1 teaspoon salt

1½ cups chopped pecans

Preheat the oven to 350° F. Grease and lightly flour two 9½ x 5½-inch loaf pans or six 5¾ x 3½-inch loaf pans.

In a large bowl, cream the butter and sugar until smooth; add the eggs and beat until light. Blend in the pumpkin and milk. In another bowl, combine the flour, spice, baking powder, soda, salt, and pecans. Add the dry ingredients to the pumpkin mixture and stir just until the flour is moistened. Turn into the prepared pans and bake for 1 hour to 1 hour and 15 minutes for the large loaves or 50 minutes to 1 hour for the smaller loaves, or until they test done. Cool 5 minutes in the pans, then turn out onto racks to finish cooling.

Makes two large or six small loaves

Cranberry Raisin Bread

❧

This moist, sweet-tart, and easy-to-make bread is perfect for holiday brunches, bazaars, and bake sales. It's great with Orange Cream Cheese Spread (page 117). It slices best the next day.

2 cups all-purpose flour

1 cup sugar

1½ teaspoons baking powder

¼ teaspoon salt

1 teaspoon grated orange peel

¼ cup (½ stick) butter, melted

1 egg, slightly beaten

¾ cup orange juice

1½ cups raisins, golden or dark

1 cup fresh or frozen cranberries, chopped

½ cup chopped pecans

Preheat the oven to 350° F. Grease one 9½ x 5½-inch loaf pan or three 5¾ x 3½-inch loaf pans.

Into a large bowl, measure all of the ingredients in the order listed. Stir just until moistened. Turn into the prepared pan or pans. Bake 35 to 45 minutes for small loaves or 1 hour for the large loaf, or until they test done. Turn out of the pan and cool on a rack.

Makes one large or three small loaves

Black Walnut
Tea Bread

❧

Black walnuts were enjoyed by Native Americans 3,000 years ago. They add a wonderful aroma to this simple quick bread. Try it with **Spiced Amaretto Butter (page 119)**.

¾ cup sugar	1½ cups milk
3 tablespoons butter, softened	2¾ cups all-purpose flour
1 egg	1 tablespoon baking powder
1 tablespoon grated lemon peel	½ teaspoon salt
	1 cup chopped black walnuts

Preheat the oven to 350° F. Grease one 9½ x 5½-inch loaf pan or three 5¾ x 3½-inch loaf pans.

In a large bowl, mix the sugar, butter, egg, lemon peel, and milk. In another bowl, stir the flour, baking powder, and salt together and add to the creamed ingredients, stirring just until moistened. Blend in the nuts. Pour into the prepared pan or pans. Bake 45 to 55 minutes for small loaves or 55 to 60 minutes for the large loaf, or until they test done. Remove from the pan and cool on a rack.

Makes one large or three small loaves

Cinnamon Pear Tea Bread

·❧·

This bread is moist and aromatic with cinnamon. Make it when pears are in season and at their tastiest.

1/4 cup (1/2 stick) butter, at room temperature
1/2 cup granulated sugar
1 egg
1/2 teaspoon vanilla extract
1 cup all-purpose flour
1/2 teaspoon baking powder

1/2 teaspoon baking soda
1/2 teaspoon ground cinnamon
1/4 teaspoon salt
1/2 cup sour cream
1 large pear, peeled and cut in 1/2-inch dice (about 1 1/2 cups)

NUT TOPPING

2 tablespoons (1/4 stick) butter or margarine, at room temperature
3/4 teaspoon ground cinnamon

1/2 cup light brown sugar, packed
1/2 cup chopped walnuts

Preheat the oven to 350° F. Grease and flour one 9 1/2 x 5 1/2-inch loaf pan or three 5 3/4 x 3 1/2-inch loaf pans.

Cream the butter and granulated sugar together until blended. Add the egg and vanilla and beat until light. Combine the flour, baking powder, soda, cinnamon, and salt in a small bowl. Add to the creamed mixture, alternately with the sour cream, mixing just to blend after each addition. Stir in the diced pear. Turn into the prepared pan or pans.

In a small bowl, make the nut topping. Blend the butter, cinnamon, brown sugar, and nuts until well combined and crumbly. Sprinkle over the dough in the pan. Bake for 40 to 45 minutes for the small loaves or 50 to 55 minutes for the large, or until they test done. Cool in the pan for 10 minutes, then turn out onto a rack and finish cooling.

Makes one large or three small loaves

Lemon-Glazed Cardamom Pear Tea Bread

❧

Cardamom brings out the flavor of pear in this tea bread. Cardamom that you buy already ground has lost most of its flavor, so I always buy whole cardamom in its white, papery pod. You just open up the pod and crush or grind the little black seeds inside. Select fully ripened, russet-skinned Bosc pears for the very best flavor.

1 cup freshly pureed ripe pears (about 2 medium, peeled and cored)

½ cup vegetable oil

1 egg, slightly beaten

2 teaspoons grated lemon peel

¼ cup milk

2½ cups all-purpose flour

½ cup granulated sugar

1 tablespoon baking powder

1 teaspoon salt

½ teaspoon freshly ground cardamom seeds

½ cup chopped walnuts or pecans

LEMON GLAZE

1 cup powdered sugar

1 tablespoon lemon juice

½ teaspoon freshly ground cardamom seeds

Dash of salt

1–2 tablespoons cream or milk

1 teaspoon butter, softened

Preheat the oven to 350° F. Grease one 9½ x 5½-inch loaf pan or three 5¾ x 3½-inch loaf pans.

In a small bowl, combine the pureed pears, oil, egg, lemon peel, and milk. In a mixing bowl, stir together the flour, sugar, baking powder, salt, and cardamom seeds. Fold in the pear mixture just until the dry ingredients are moistened. Stir in the nuts. Spoon the dough into the prepared pan or pans. Bake 55 to 60 minutes for a large loaf or 35 to 45 minutes for smaller loaves, or until they test done. Remove from the pan and cool on a rack.

While the bread bakes, stir together the glaze ingredients. Spoon the glaze over the still-warm bread. Continue to cool.

Makes one large or three small loaves

Cheddar
Apple Bread

❧

This bread is delicious fresh
from the oven, but try it made into French toast.

½ cup (1 stick) butter, at
  room temperature
¾ cup sugar
2 eggs
1¾ cups all-purpose flour
1 teaspoon baking powder
½ teaspoon baking soda
½ teaspoon salt

½ teaspoon ground cinnamon
¼ teaspoon freshly ground
  nutmeg
1 cup chopped tart apple (1
  medium, peeled and cored)
½ cup shredded sharp
  Cheddar cheese
⅓ cup chopped pecans

Preheat the oven to 350° F. Grease and flour one 9½ x 5½-inch loaf pan or three 5¾ x 3½-inch loaf pans.

In a large mixing bowl, cream the butter and sugar; add the eggs and beat until light. Stir the flour, baking powder, soda, salt, cinnamon, and nutmeg together. Add with the apple to the creamed mixture. Fold in the cheese and pecans. Turn into the prepared pan or pans. Bake 1 hour for a large loaf, 40 to 45 minutes for small loaves, or until they test done. Cool in the pan for 5 minutes, then turn out onto a rack to finish cooling.

Makes one large or three small loaves

Zucchini
Walnut Bread

❧

In a quick bread, zucchini
adds a pretty, confettilike fleck as well as moistness and
flavor.

1½ cups all-purpose flour	2 eggs, beaten
1½ teaspoons ground cinnamon	1 cup sugar
	1½ teaspoons vanilla extract
½ teaspoon salt	½ cup vegetable oil
1 teaspoon baking powder	1½ cups shredded zucchini
½ teaspoon baking soda	½ cup chopped black walnuts

Preheat the oven to 350° F. Grease a 9½ x 5½-inch loaf pan or
three 5¾ x 3½-inch loaf pans.

In a medium bowl, stir together the flour, cinnamon, salt,
baking powder, and soda. In another bowl, beat the eggs with
the sugar, vanilla, and vegetable oil until thick. Fold the dry
ingredients into the beaten mixture until well blended. Stir in
the zucchini and the nuts. Pour into the prepared loaf pan or
pans and bake 1 hour for the large loaf or 40 to 45 minutes for
small loaves, or until they test done. Remove from the pan and
cool on a rack.

Makes one large or three small loaves

Date Nut Cranberry Bread

✿

Keep a loaf of this bread on hand in the freezer—it makes great, unusual turkey sandwiches. Just spread with cream cheese, top with thinly sliced plain or smoked turkey breast, and garnish with a dab of cranberry sauce.

2 cups all-purpose flour

2 teaspoons baking powder

½ teaspoon baking soda

¼ teaspoon salt

4 tablespoons (½ stick) butter

¾ cup sugar

1 cup chopped walnuts

1 tablespoon grated orange rind

1 egg

⅔ cup orange juice

1 cup fresh raw cranberries, chopped

1 cup chopped dates

GLAZE

1 tablespoon milk

1 tablespoon sugar

Preheat the oven to 350° F. Grease and flour a 9½ x 5½-inch loaf pan or three 5¾ x 3½-inch loaf pans.

In a large bowl, stir the flour, baking powder, soda, and salt together. With a fork or pastry blender, cut in the butter until the mixture is crumbly. Stir in the sugar, walnuts, and orange rind. In a small bowl, whisk the egg and orange juice together and stir into the dry ingredients just until blended; the mixture will be lumpy. Blend in the cranberries and dates. Spoon into the prepared pan or pans.

To glaze, smooth the top of the loaf or loaves and brush with the milk, then sprinkle with the sugar. Bake 45 to 55 minutes for small loaves or 1 hour to 1 hour 15 minutes for the large loaf, or until they test done. Remove from the oven and cool in the pan for 10 minutes. Turn out onto a rack to finish cooling.

Makes one large or three small loaves

Prune
Walnut Bread

⚶

Sherry-soaked prunes dot
the golden crumb of this bread. It's delicious hot, but
slices better after it has cooled.

1 cup pitted prunes, chopped

1/4 cup dry Sherry

1/2 cup (1 stick) butter, at
room temperature

1 cup sugar

2 eggs, at room temperature

1 tablespoon grated lemon
rind

2 cups all-purpose flour

2 teaspoons baking powder

1 teaspoon salt

1/2 cup milk

1 cup coarsely chopped
walnuts

In a small bowl, combine the prunes and Sherry; set aside to
soak for 30 minutes.

Preheat the oven to 350° F. Grease one 9½ x 5½-inch loaf
pan or three 5¾ x 3½-inch loaf pans.

In a large mixing bowl, cream the butter and sugar; add the
eggs and lemon rind and beat until light and fluffy. In another
bowl, stir the flour, baking powder, and salt together. Add to
the creamed mixture alternately with the milk. Stir just until
moistened. Fold in the prunes, with their liquid, and the nuts.
Turn into the prepared pan or pans. Bake 1 hour for the large

loaf or 40 to 45 minutes for small loaves, or until they test done. Cool 5 minutes in the pan, then turn out onto a rack to cool completely.

Makes one large or three small loaves

Pistachio Nut Bread

❧

Native to Asia Minor and green in their natural state, pistachios are also grown in the Southwestern United States. Usually eaten as a snack or tucked into ice cream, they're wonderful baked into this bread, too!

½ cup (1 stick) butter, at room temperature

¾ cup granulated sugar

2 eggs

¼ cup fresh lemon juice

1 tablespoon grated lemon rind

1½ cups all-purpose flour

1 tablespoon baking powder

⅛ teaspoon salt

½ cup milk

1 cup chopped pistachios

GLAZE

2 tablespoons fresh lemon juice

½ cup powdered sugar

Preheat the oven to 350° F. Grease and flour one 9½ x 5½-inch loaf pan or three 5¾ x 3½-inch loaf pans.

In a large mixing bowl, cream the butter and granulated sugar until well blended. Beat in the eggs, lemon juice, and lemon rind until the mixture is fluffy. In another bowl, stir the flour, baking powder, and salt together and add to the creamed mixture alternately with the milk. Fold in the pistachios; stir until blended. Turn into the prepared pan or pans. Bake 60 to 65 minutes for a large loaf or 40 to 45 minutes for small loaves, or until they test done.

Meanwhile, in a small bowl, stir together the lemon juice and powdered sugar until smooth. Poke holes in the top of the hot bread with a wooden skewer and drizzle the glaze evenly over it. Cool in the pan 5 minutes; turn out onto a rack to cool completely.

Makes one large or three small loaves

DARK AND
RICH BREADS

❧

Mincemeat Apricot Bread

Favorite Date Nut Bread

Carrot Walnut Bread

Granola Chocolate Cherry Bread

Fruited Apple Loaf

Cheddar Date Nut Loaf

Whole-Wheat Walnut Banana Bread

Toasted-Coconut Rum Banana Bread

Bishop's Bread

Oat Bran Date Nut Bread

Mincemeat Apricot Bread

❧

Dense, dark, and moist describes this fruity bread. Though it's delicious fresh from the oven, it improves with age. This is a great bread to make and wrap as gifts because it makes so many little loaves.

1 cup (6-ounce package) dried apricots, chopped

1 cup (6-ounce package) condensed, dry mincemeat (see note)

2 cups water

1 cup sugar

2 tablespoons (¼ stick) butter

1 egg

1 tablespoon grated orange rind

3½ cups all-purpose flour

3 teaspoons baking powder

1 teaspoon baking soda

1 teaspoon salt

½ cup buttermilk

½ cup orange juice

¼ cup chopped walnuts

Preheat the oven to 375° F. Grease and flour two 9½ x 5½-inch loaf pans or six 5¾ x 3½-inch loaf pans.

In a saucepan, combine the apricots, mincemeat, and water. Place over high heat and bring to a boil. Adjust the heat to low, cover, and cook until the apricots are tender, about 20 minutes. Remove from the heat and cool.

In a large mixing bowl, cream the sugar and butter; beat in the egg and orange rind. Measure the flour, baking powder, soda, and salt into the bowl. Pour the buttermilk, orange juice, cooked fruit, and walnuts over the top. Stir just until the dry ingredients are moistened. Spoon into the prepared pans. Bake 1 hour for large loaves or 45 to 55 minutes for the smaller loaves, or until they test done. Cool in the pans for 5 minutes, then turn out onto racks to finish cooling.

NOTE: Condensed mincemeat comes in a package rather than a jar; it is dry and compact, and must be crumbled. You can substitute ½ cup ground dried apples, ½ cup ground dark raisins, 1 teaspoon cinnamon, 1 teaspoon nutmeg, and 1 teaspoon cloves, if you wish.

Makes two large or six small loaves

Favorite Date Nut Bread

❧

Date nut bread always makes me think of Thanksgiving—perhaps because it was the first thing we baked in preparation for the holiday season, and that was usually the week of Thanksgiving. This is a moist dark-colored loaf that keeps well. It will slice the best the day after it's made. I like it with a thinly shaved slice of sharp Cheddar cheese.

1 cup pitted dates, chopped
1 teaspoon baking soda
2 tablespoons (¼ stick) butter
1 cup boiling water
1 egg
⅓ cup granulated sugar

⅓ cup brown sugar, packed
2½ cups all-purpose flour
1 teaspoon baking powder
¼ teaspoon salt
1 cup coarsely chopped walnuts

Preheat the oven to 350° F. Grease and flour one 9½ x 5½-inch loaf pan or three 5¾ x 3½-inch loaf pans.

In a medium bowl, combine the dates, soda, butter, and boiling water. Set aside to cool to room temperature.

In a large mixing bowl, beat the egg until frothy; beat in the sugars until fluffy. In another bowl, stir the flour, baking powder, and salt together and add to the egg mixture alternately with the date mixture, stirring just until the flour is moistened. Fold in the nuts. Spoon into the prepared pan or pans and bake 1 hour for the large loaf or 35 to 45 minutes for the small loaves, or until they test done. Cool in the pan for 5 minutes, then turn onto a rack to finish cooling.

Makes one large or three small loaves

Carrot Walnut Bread

❧

This bread falls somewhere between golden and dark and rich. It is especially good toasted with a slice of Monterey Jack cheese.

2 cups all-purpose flour
1 cup chopped walnuts
½ cup granulated sugar
½ cup brown sugar, packed
3 teaspoons baking powder
1 teaspoon ground cinnamon
½ teaspoon salt
2 cups finely shredded fresh carrots
½ cup milk
⅓ cup vegetable oil
1 egg

Preheat the oven to 350° F. Grease and flour one 9½ x 5½-inch loaf pan or three 5¾ x 3½-inch loaf pans.

In a large mixing bowl, combine the flour, nuts, sugars, baking powder, cinnamon, and salt until well blended. Stir in the remaining ingredients just until moistened. Spoon into pan or pans. Bake 50 to 60 minutes for a large loaf, 35 to 45 minutes for small loaves, or until they test done. Cool in the pan for 10 minutes, then turn out onto a rack to finish cooling.

Makes one large or three small loaves

Granola Chocolate Cherry Bread

❧

This pretty, festive-looking bread is sure to please chocolate lovers.

1⅓ cups all-purpose flour

⅓ cup sugar

1 teaspoon baking soda

½ teaspoon salt

1 cup buttermilk

⅓ cup vegetable oil

1 teaspoon vanilla extract

1 egg

1 cup granola breakfast cereal

½ cup chopped almonds

½ cup semisweet mini chocolate chips

¾ cup chopped candied cherries

Preheat the oven to 350° F. Grease and flour an 8½ x 4½-inch loaf pan.

In a medium mixing bowl, stir together the flour, sugar, baking soda, and salt. In a large mixing bowl, blend the buttermilk, oil, vanilla, and egg. Stir in the dry ingredients just until blended. Fold in the granola, almonds, chocolate chips, and cherries. Spoon into the prepared pan. Bake for 55 to 60 minutes, or until it tests done. Let cool in the pan for 10 minutes, remove, and finish cooling on a rack.

Makes one medium loaf

Fruited
Apple Loaf

This is terrific for the holidays, a cross between a nut bread and an aged fruitcake, but less dense. Keep the loaves wrapped and refrigerated up to a month. Cut in thin slices and spread with fruit-flavored cream cheese (page 117 or 118).

1 cup light or dark brown sugar, packed

½ cup vegetable oil

2 tablespoons Sherry

2 eggs

1 teaspoon vanilla extract

1 cup light or dark raisins

1 cup coarsely chopped mixed candied fruits

1 cup chopped walnuts or pecans

1 cup pitted chopped dates

1½ cups chopped tart apple (about 3 small, peeled and cored)

2 teaspoons baking soda

2 cups all-purpose flour

½ teaspoon salt

½ teaspoon ground cinnamon

¼ teaspoon freshly ground nutmeg

Preheat the oven to 350° F. Grease and flour one 9½ x 5½-inch loaf pan or three 5¾ x 3½-inch loaf pans.

In a large mixing bowl, combine the brown sugar, oil, Sherry, eggs, vanilla, raisins, fruits, nuts, and dates. In a small bowl, stir the apples and baking soda together and add to the fruit-nut mixture. In another bowl, stir the flour, salt, cinnamon, and nutmeg together and blend into the fruit mixture.

Spoon into the prepared pan or pans and bake 1 hour and 25 minutes for the large loaf or 50 to 60 minutes for the smaller loaves, or until they test done. Cool 5 minutes in the pan, then turn out onto a rack to finish cooling.

Makes one large or three small loaves

Cheddar Date
Nut Loaf

৯৬

With sharp Cheddar cheese baked right in, this loaf is moist, dense, and richly flavored, and even better the next day. For a connoisseur's dessert, slice it thin and serve with chilled white Port.

8 ounces (about 1½ cups) pitted, chopped dates	¼ teaspoon salt
¾ cup boiling water	½ cup sugar
2 tablespoons (¼ stick) butter	1 egg, lightly beaten
1¾ cups all-purpose flour	1 cup shredded sharp Cheddar cheese
2 teaspoons baking powder	1 cup walnuts, coarsely chopped
½ teaspoon baking soda	

Preheat the oven to 350° F. Grease and flour one 9½ x 5½-inch loaf pan or three 5¾ x 3½-inch loaf pans.

In a medium bowl, combine the dates, boiling water, and butter. Set aside to cool to room temperature. In a large bowl, stir together the flour, baking powder, soda, salt, and sugar. Add the date mixture and egg. Stir in the cheese and nuts just until blended.

Spoon the mixture into the prepared pan or pans and bake 45 minutes for the smaller loaves or 50 to 60 minutes for the large loaf, or until they test done. Cool in the pan for 5 minutes, then turn out onto a rack and finish cooling. Refrigerate until serving.

Makes one large or three small loaves

Whole-Wheat Walnut Banana Bread

೩

When bananas turn black, I often whirl them in the blender, pack in 1-cup batches in heavy-duty plastic bags, and freeze. I thaw the fruit, in the bag, in a bowl of warm water.

½ cup (1 stick) butter, at room temperature	1 cup all-purpose flour
1 cup sugar	1 cup whole-wheat flour
2 eggs	1 teaspoon baking powder
1 cup mashed ripe bananas (about 3 medium)	½ teaspoon baking soda
	½ teaspoon salt
	½ cup chopped walnuts

Preheat the oven to 350° F. Grease and flour one 9½ x 5½-inch loaf pan or three 5¾ x 3½-inch loaf pans.

In a large mixing bowl, cream the butter and sugar until well blended. Beat in the eggs and mashed banana. In a small bowl, combine the flours, baking powder, soda, and salt and blend into the creamed mixture. Stir in the nuts. Turn into the prepared pan or pans. Bake 1 hour and 10 minutes for the large loaf or 45 to 55 minutes for the smaller loaves, or until they test done. Cool in the pan 5 minutes, then remove to a rack and finish cooling.

Makes one large or three small loaves

Toasted-Coconut Rum Banana Bread

🍌

I patterned this bread after one we enjoyed in Barbados, where coconuts, rum, and bananas are abundant.

½ cup (1 stick) butter, at
    room temperature
⅔ cup sugar
2 eggs
3 tablespoons dark rum
½ teaspoon almond extract
2 cups all-purpose flour
1 teaspoon baking powder

½ teaspoon baking soda
½ teaspoon salt
1 cup mashed ripe banana
    (about 3 medium)
1 cup flaked coconut, toasted
    5–8 minutes in a 350° F.
    oven

Preheat the oven to 350° F. Grease and flour a 9½ x 5½-inch loaf pan or three 5¾ x 3½-inch loaf pans.

In a large mixing bowl, cream the butter and sugar. Beat in the eggs, rum, and almond extract. In another bowl, stir the flour, baking powder, soda, and salt together, then add to the creamed mixture. Blend in the banana and coconut. Turn into the prepared pan or pans. Bake 55 to 60 minutes for the large loaf or 45 to 55 minutes for the smaller loaves, or until they test done. Cool in the pan 5 minutes, then turn onto a rack.

Makes one large or three small loaves

Bishop's Bread

❧

Legend has it that this bread comes from the 19th-century American frontier when settlements would be visited by traveling clergymen. A hostess invented this recipe when a bishop dropped in unexpectedly one Sunday morning. All I can say is that she must have been a fast worker, peeling the apples and chopping them along with the walnuts and dates, unless she enlisted the help of the bishop! I enriched the recipe with chocolate chips.

¼ cup (½ stick) butter	½ cup chopped dates
1 square (1 ounce) unsweetened chocolate	1 cup chopped tart apple (1 medium, peeled and cored)
2 cups all-purpose flour	⅓ cup semisweet mini chocolate chips
½ cup sugar	2 eggs
3½ teaspoons baking powder	1 cup milk
½ teaspoon salt	
½ cup chopped walnuts	

Preheat the oven to 350° F. Grease one 9½ x 5½-inch loaf pan or three 5¾ x 3½-inch loaf pans.

In a small saucepan, combine the butter and chocolate. Place over low heat until melted. In a large bowl, stir together the flour, sugar, baking powder, and salt. Add the walnuts, dates, apple, and chocolate chips. In a small bowl, beat the eggs and milk together; blend them into the flour mixture. Stir in the melted butter and chocolate, blending well. Turn into the prepared pan. Bake for 1 hour for the large loaf or 45 to 55 minutes for the smaller loaves, or until the loaves are brown and they test done. Remove from the pan, cut into thick slices, and serve warm.

Makes one large or three small loaves

Oat Bran
Date Nut Bread

❧

Oat bran has been the darling of the health-food media recently, but you can substitute uncooked rolled oats if you pulverize them first: Measure the oats into a blender or a food processor with the steel blade in place, and process until coarse but not completely powdered. If your diet requires, use margarine instead of butter and egg whites in place of whole eggs.

1 cup boiling water
1½ cups pitted, chopped dates
½ cup (1 stick) butter (or margarine)
2 tablespoons grated orange rind
1 cup fresh orange juice
2 eggs (or 3 egg whites)
2 cups all-purpose flour

2 cups oat bran or chopped rolled oats
¾ cup light brown sugar, packed
2 teaspoons baking powder
2 teaspoons baking soda
¾ teaspoon salt
1 cup coarsely chopped walnuts

Preheat the oven to 350° F. Grease and flour two 8½ x 4½-inch loaf pans.

In a medium bowl, pour the boiling water over the dates and butter. Set aside to cool to room temperature. Stir in the orange rind, juice, and eggs; blend well. In a large mixing bowl, combine the flour, oat bran, sugar, baking powder, soda, salt, and walnuts. Add the date mixture and stir just until moistened. Pour the batter into the prepared pans. Bake for about 1 hour 20 minutes, or until bread pulls away from the sides of the pans and they test done. Let cool in the pans for 10 minutes, then turn onto a rack to finish cooling.

Makes two medium loaves

SAVORY QUICK BREADS

Boston Brown Bread

Colonial Brown Bread

Buttermilk Apple Brown Bread

Yogurt Nut Brown Bread

Finnish Barley Bread

Herbed Irish Soda Bread

Caraway Beer Bread

Cheese Supper Bread

Hot Raisin Bread

Australian Damper

Boston Brown Bread

❧

You can steam this brown bread in a number of different containers. A steamed-pudding mold works well, as do coffee cans or tomato-sauce cans. Sometimes I steam it in the small 6- or 8-ounce jelly glasses that have plastic snap-top lids; they are slightly narrower on the bottom than on the top and don't have a lip to catch the bread as you un-mold it. Pint-size canning jars work well, too, if they are completely smooth and straight on the inside so you can unmold the bread well.

1 cup all-purpose flour	½ teaspoon salt
1 cup stone-ground yellow cornmeal	1½ cups buttermilk
	⅓ cup dark molasses
1 teaspoon baking soda	⅓ cup raisins

Have ready a large kettle with a cover. Place a rack in the bottom of the kettle and bring about 2 inches of water to a boil. Generously grease a 1-pound steamed-pudding mold or coffee can, six 8-ounce containers, or 3 pint containers.

In a large mixing bowl, stir the flour, cornmeal, baking soda, and salt until blended. Add the buttermilk, molasses, and raisins.

Mix until well blended. Spoon the batter into the prepared containers, filling each ⅔ full. Cover tightly with foil.

Place the cans in the kettle so the boiling water comes halfway up the sides. Cover the kettle and steam 1 hour for half-pint and pint-size containers, or 2 hours for a large 1-pound container or mold, or until they test done. Add more water as necessary during cooking. Cool, then unmold.

Makes one 1-pound loaf, 6 small (8-ounce) loaves, or 3 loaves baked in pint-size canning jars

Colonial
Brown Bread

❧

So simple, so hearty and satisfying, this is a bread to serve with an old-fashioned pot roast or stew in the wintertime after skiing. There is no shortening or egg in the mixture.

2 cups buttermilk

2 cups whole-wheat flour

⅔ cup all-purpose flour

½ cup light-brown sugar, packed

2 teaspoons baking soda

1 teaspoon pumpkin-pie spice

½ teaspoon salt

¾ cup raisins (optional)

Preheat the oven to 350° F. Grease a 9½ x 5½-inch loaf pan.

In a large bowl, combine all of the ingredients and stir until blended. Spoon into the prepared pan. Bake for 1 hour, or until it tests done. Remove from the pan and cool on a rack. Cut into thick slices while still warm.

Makes one large loaf

Buttermilk Apple Brown Bread

୬

This moist, compact bread tastes rich even though it has only 3 tablespoons of butter. It's great with a vegetable soup or a salad for a light supper.

3 tablespoons butter, softened	2 teaspoons baking soda
¾ cup brown sugar, packed	1 teaspoon salt
2 cups buttermilk	1 cup finely chopped tart
3 tablespoons light molasses	apple (1 medium, peeled
2 cups whole-wheat flour	and cored)
1 cup all-purpose flour	½ cup raisins
½ cup old-fashioned rolled oats	1 cup chopped walnuts

Preheat oven to 350° F. Grease two 8½ x 4½-inch loaf pans.

In a large bowl, mix the butter, brown sugar, buttermilk, and molasses. In another bowl, combine the flours, rolled oats, soda, and salt. Add the dry ingredients to the liquid ingredients and stir just until blended. Stir in the apple, raisins, and walnuts. Spoon the dough into the prepared pans and smooth the tops. Bake for 60 to 70 minutes, or until they test done. Cool for 10 minutes in the pans, then remove and cool on a rack.

Makes two medium loaves

Yogurt Nut Brown Bread

ℐ

It's compact, dark, grainy,
and rich-tasting—yet there's no fat or egg in this loaf!

1 cup stone-ground rye flour	1 teaspoon salt
1 cup whole-wheat flour	2 cups plain yogurt
½ cup all-purpose flour	⅓ cup light molasses
2 teaspoons baking soda	½ cup chopped walnuts

Preheat the oven to 350° F. Grease one 9½ x 5½-inch loaf pan
or three 5¾ x 3½-inch loaf pans.

In a large bowl, stir together the flours, baking soda, and salt.
In another bowl, stir together the yogurt and molasses. Blend
the yogurt mixture into the dry ingredients and stir in the walnuts just until all the ingredients are moistened. Spoon into the
prepared pan or pans. Bake 1 hour for the large loaf or 35 to
45 minutes for the smaller loaves, or until they test done. Remove from the oven, let cool in the pan for 10 minutes, then
turn onto a rack to finish cooling.

Makes one large or three small loaves

Finnish Barley Bread

❧

You'll marvel at how quick this bread is to make and how delicious it is either fresh from the oven or cooled. Cut it into 8 wedges and serve it with sweet butter or sliced Emmenthaler cheese.

2 cups barley flour	¾ teaspoon salt
2 teaspoons baking powder	2 cups light cream or
2 teaspoons sugar	half-and-half

Preheat the oven to 450° F. Grease a 12-inch pizza pan or a 12-inch round baking sheet.

Stir together all of the ingredients to make a stiff dough. Turn out onto the prepared baking sheet. With flour-dusted hands, pat the dough into an evenly thick circle. Puncture it all over with a fork. Bake for 10 minutes, or until the bread feels firm and dry on the top but is not crisp. Remove from the oven and serve immediately.

Makes one 12-inch round flat loaf

Herbed Irish Soda Bread

❧

This is superb hot or cold, though it won't slice well the day it's made. It has an even richer herb flavor when toasted that's perfect with potato or vegetable soup.

3 cups all-purpose flour	1 teaspoon dried or fresh
½ teaspoon salt	thyme
2½ teaspoons baking powder	2 tablespoons butter
½ teaspoon baking soda	1 egg
2 tablespoons sugar	¾ cup buttermilk

Preheat the oven to 375° F. Grease an 8-inch round cake pan or pie pan.

In a large bowl, stir together the flour, salt, baking powder, soda, sugar, and thyme. With a fork or pastry blender, cut the butter into the dry ingredients until crumbly. In a small bowl, mix the egg and buttermilk, then stir into the dry ingredients. Turn out onto a lightly floured board and knead until smooth, 2 to 3 minutes. Shape into a smooth round loaf. Press into the prepared baking pan. With a sharp knife, cut a long X on top of the loaf. Bake 35 to 40 minutes, or just until golden.

Makes one 8-inch round loaf

Caraway
Beer Bread

୬ଚ

This stirs up very quickly
and results in a rather coarse-grained, rustic loaf. With
Herbed Chèvre Spread (page 114), it's a perfect accompaniment to hearty soups or stews, and just as great
with barbecued meats and poultry.

3½ cups self-rising flour (see
   note)
1 tablespoon sugar

1 tablespoon caraway seeds
1 tablespoon vegetable oil
1 (12-ounce) can beer

Preheat the oven to 375° F. Lightly butter an 8-inch or 9-inch
round cake pan.

In a large bowl, mix all of the ingredients in the order given
until moist. Turn into the cake pan. Bake for 45 to 55 minutes,
or until it tests done. Remove from the pan and serve warm.

NOTE: Self-rising flour has leavening and salt added to it.
If desired, you may use 3½ cups all-purpose flour, 3½ teaspoons baking powder, and 1 teaspoon salt instead.

Makes one 8-inch or 9-inch round loaf

Cheese Supper Bread

❧

This is a quick-to-mix bread baked in a pie pan. Use your favorite medium-hard cheese, or even a combination; this is a delicious way to use up any leftover cheeses you have on hand.

1 ½ cups all-purpose flour

2 teaspoons baking powder

¼ teaspoon salt

2 tablespoons vegetable oil

1 egg

¼ cup milk

1 cup (4 ounces) shredded cheese (Swiss, Cheddar, and Muenster work best)

2 tablespoons (¼ stick) butter, melted

1 teaspoon poppy seeds

Preheat the oven to 400° F. Grease a 9-inch pie pan.

In a mixing bowl, combine the flour, baking powder, salt, oil, egg, milk, and ½ cup of cheese. Stir just until the dry ingredients are moistened; the dough will be stiff but sticky. Transfer it to a 9-inch pie pan and, with floured hands, pat it evenly into the bottom. Drizzle with the melted butter and evenly sprinkle the remaining cheese and the poppy seeds over the top. Bake for 20 to 25 minutes, or until lightly browned. Cut into wedges and serve hot.

Makes one 9-inch round loaf

Hot Raisin Bread

❧

Here's another quick-to-mix—and bake—bread. It's best hot out of the oven and is just right for afternoon tea or morning coffee.

2 cups all-purpose flour

2 teaspoons baking powder

1/4 teaspoon salt

1/4 cup vegetable oil

3/4 cup milk

1/3 cup golden or dark raisins

2 tablespoons sugar

2 tablespoons (1/4 stick) butter, melted or soft

1/4 cup cinnamon sugar (1/4 cup sugar plus 1/2 teaspoon cinnamon)

Preheat the oven to 450° F. Grease a baking sheet or cover with parchment paper.

In a mixing bowl, combine the flour, baking powder, salt, oil, milk, raisins, and sugar, and mix into a soft dough. Transfer it to the baking sheet and, with floured hands, pat the dough into an 8-inch square, about 1/2-inch thick. Spread with the butter and sprinkle with the cinnamon sugar. Bake for 10 to 12 minutes, or until just golden. Cut into squares and serve hot.

Makes one 8-inch square loaf

Australian Damper

❧

Originally, "damper" was made from only flour and water, and was the bread that sustained stockmen, squatters, and bushrangers in Australia's early days. It was baked directly on hot ashes, dusted off, and eaten with its charred crust. This is a modern version made with leavening and herbs added to the dough. (For a more authentic bread, omit the herbs.) It's wonderful served warm with Herbed Chèvre Spread (page 114) or cut into thick slices and toasted for breakfast.

3 cups plus one tablespoon all-purpose flour

4 teaspoons baking powder

1 teaspoon salt

¼ cup (½ stick) cold butter, cut into small pieces

2 tablespoons chopped fresh herbs (thyme, rosemary, oregano)

½ cup plus one tablespoon milk

½ cup water

Preheat the oven to 400° F. Lightly grease an 8-inch cake pan or a baking sheet.

In a mixing bowl, stir 3 cups of the flour, the baking powder, and salt together. With a pastry blender or fork, cut in the butter until the mixture resembles coarse meal. Stir in the herbs,

½ cup of the milk, and water to make a stiff dough. Turn out onto a lightly floured surface and knead a few times to make a smooth ball. Pat the dough into a circle that will fit into the cake pan, or place it on the greased baking sheet.

Cut two slits in the top about ½-inch deep. Brush the top with the remaining tablespoon of milk and dust generously with the tablespoon of flour. Bake for 30 minutes, or until it tests done. Serve warm.

Makes one 8-inch round loaf

STICKS, ROLLS, AND CORN BREADS

Cinnamon Raisin Rolls

Quick Cheese Croissants

Corn Puffs

Corn and Rice Sticks

Quick Cardamom Buns

Honey Pecan Corn Sticks

Buttermilk Corn Bread

Soufflé Spoon Bread

Cheese-Topped Corn Bread

Hot Pepper and Bacon Corn Bread

Yankee Corn Bread

Cracklin' Corn Bread

Cinnamon Raisin Rolls

❧

These quick rolls are filled with a buttery mixture of raisins, brown sugar, and cinnamon. If you place the rolls close together in a pan, it turns out to be a coffee bread. Baked separately on a baking sheet, they are individual rolls.

3½ cups all-purpose flour
4 teaspoons baking powder
1 teaspoon salt

½ cup (1 stick) cold butter, cut into small pieces
2 eggs, beaten
¾ to 1 cup milk

FILLING

½ cup (1 stick) butter, softened
½ cup brown sugar, packed

1½ cups golden or dark raisins
1½ teaspoons ground cinnamon

GLAZE

1½ tablespoons granulated sugar
1½ tablespoons water

1½ teaspoons unflavored gelatin

Preheat the oven to 400° F. Grease a 9-inch springform pan, square pan, or 10-inch tube pan, or cover a baking sheet with parchment paper.

In a bowl, combine the flour, baking powder, and salt. Cut the cold butter into the mixture with a fork or pastry blender until the mixture resembles coarse meal. In a small bowl, combine the eggs and milk, and mix into the flour, using a fork to make a soft dough.

Gather the dough into a ball and, on a lightly floured surface, roll it out to make a 12-inch square about ¼-inch thick. Spread with the softened butter and sprinkle evenly with the brown sugar, raisins, and cinnamon. Roll up and cut into 8 equal pieces about 1½-inches long. Place into the prepared pan. If using a springform or tube pan, the pieces will touch. On a baking sheet, arrange the pieces apart so they will bake separately. Bake for 20 to 25 minutes for rolls on a baking sheet, or 35 to 40 minutes for bread baked in a pan.

For the glaze, combine the granulated sugar, water, and gelatin in a small bowl. Set over boiling water and stir until the mixture is clear. Brush the hot rolls with the glaze.

Makes 8 large rolls

Quick Cheese Croissants

❧

Cottage cheese and Cheddar cheese in the dough make these unconventional croissants rich and flaky.

2 cups all-purpose flour
3 teaspoons baking powder
½ teaspoon salt
¼ cup (½ stick) cold butter, cut into small pieces
½ cup creamed cottage cheese

1 cup (4 ounces) shredded sharp Cheddar cheese
1 egg
¼ cup milk
3 tablespoons melted butter
1 egg, beaten, for glaze

Preheat the oven to 425° F. Lightly grease a baking sheet or cover it with parchment paper.

In a bowl, combine the flour, baking powder, and salt. With a pastry blender or fork, cut in the butter until the mixture resembles coarse meal, then work in the cheeses until blended. Add the egg and enough milk to form a soft dough. Divide the dough into 4 equal parts and shape each into a ball. On a lightly floured surface, roll each ball out to make a round about 10 inches across and ¼-inch thick. Cut each round into 4 equal wedges. (For appetizer-size croissants, cut into 8 wedges.) Brush the rounds with melted butter.

Starting with the long edge of each wedge, roll up toward the point of the wedge and twist into a crescent. Place on the prepared baking sheet with the tip of each wedge pointing to the bottom. Brush with the beaten egg. Bake for 10 to 12 minutes, or until pale golden brown. Serve hot with butter or a savory spread.

Makes 16 croissants

Corn Puffs

These delightfully crunchy little cornmeal puffs look like drop cookies. They are the perfect accompaniment for a creamy soup.

½ cup yellow cornmeal
¼ teaspoon salt

½ cup boiling water
2 egg whites

Preheat the oven to 375° F. Generously grease a baking sheet.

Combine the cornmeal and salt in a bowl. Pour the boiling water over the mixture, stir, and cool.

Whip the egg whites until stiff and blend into the cornmeal mixture. Drop by teaspoonfuls on the prepared baking sheet. Bake for 30 minutes, or until the puffs are delicately browned and crispy. Serve hot with butter.

Makes 24 two-inch puffs

Corn and Rice Sticks

❧

The seemingly long baking time gives these corn sticks a crispy, thick exterior. Bag them up and freeze them, so you can take them out one at a time and pop into the microwave oven for about 30 seconds each to go with a bowl of chili.

2 cups white cornmeal	3 eggs, well beaten
1 teaspoon salt	1 cup cold cooked rice
3 teaspoons baking powder	2 tablespoons (¼ stick)
1½ cups milk	melted butter

Preheat the oven to 425° F., and put the corn-stick pans in the oven to preheat.

In a mixing bowl, stir together the cornmeal, salt, and baking powder. In another bowl, mix the milk, eggs, rice, and melted butter together. Whisk the mixture into the dry ingredients until well blended.

For a nice crust, brush the preheated pans with more melted butter (or use vegetable oil or spray). Pour the batter into the pans and bake for 30 minutes or until golden.

Makes 21 corn sticks

Quick
Cardamom Buns

✌

Cardamom is one of my favorite flavors in baked goods, but because it loses its flavor so quickly, it isn't worth buying if it's already ground in the jar. Crack open whole pods and remove the little black seeds. Grind or pulverize them in a mortar and pestle, a spice mill, or a mini electric grinder. These buns are especially good split and toasted when they are a day old.

1 ½ cups all-purpose flour	¼ cup (½ stick) butter, melted
2 teaspoons baking powder	1 egg, beaten
½ teaspoon salt	⅓ cup milk
1 ½ teaspoons cardamom seeds, freshly ground	½ teaspoon vanilla extract
¼ cup sugar	

Preheat the oven to 400° F. Lightly grease a baking sheet or cover it with parchment paper. (I prefer the parchment paper.)

In a large bowl, combine the flour, baking powder, salt, cardamom, and sugar. Make a well in the center of the dry ingredients and pour in the butter, egg, milk, and vanilla. Stir the liquids just to blend (right in the well), then quickly stir them into the dry ingredients. Do not overmix. Drop the dough into

10 mounds on the baking sheet. Bake for 12 minutes, or until golden. Cool briefly in the pans, then transfer with a spatula to racks to cool to desired temperature. Serve warm or cooled, split and buttered.

Makes 10 buns

Honey Pecan Corn Sticks

❧

The combination of pecans and honey syrup makes these corn sticks truly irresistible. If you wish, you can bake these sticks in muffin pans. My corn-stick pan bakes 7 sticks at a time. Unless you have two pans, you'll have to do as I do and bake the batter in two batches.

½ cup brown sugar, packed
2 tablespoons honey
2 tablespoons (¼ stick) butter
½ cup all-purpose flour
½ cup stone-ground yellow, white, or blue cornmeal
1 tablespoon sugar
2 teaspoons baking powder
¼ teaspoon salt
½ cup milk
2 tablespoons (¼ stick) butter, melted
1 egg, slightly beaten
¾ cup plus 2 tablespoons chopped pecans

Preheat the oven to 425° F., and put the corn-stick pans in the oven to preheat.

In a small pan, combine the brown sugar, honey, and 2 tablespoons butter; stir over low heat until the mixture boils and the sugar is dissolved. Set the syrup aside.

In a mixing bowl, combine the flour, cornmeal, sugar, baking powder, and salt until blended. Add the milk, melted butter, and egg all at once, then stir just until smooth. Brush the pre-heated pans with a thin coating of shortening or butter. Sprinkle 1 tablespoon chopped pecans into each of the corn-stick forms, then fill ⅔ full with batter. Bake for 15 to 20 minutes, or until lightly browned. Remove from the forms and drizzle with the honey syrup.

VARIATION: *Jalapeño Corn Sticks:* Add 1 finely diced, seeded jalapeño pepper to the batter. Omit the honey syrup and pecans.

Makes 14 corn sticks

Buttermilk Corn Bread

❧

White cornmeal is preferred in the American South and Midwest, while in the East and North, yellow cornmeal is the easiest to find. In either case, the stone-ground variety is usually finer, resulting in a bread that is moist and cakelike.

2 tablespoons (¼ stick) butter
2 cups stone-ground cornmeal
1 teaspoon salt
½ teaspoon baking soda
½ cup all-purpose flour
1 tablespoon sugar
2 teaspoons baking powder
1 egg
1¼ cups buttermilk

Preheat the oven to 425° F. Melt the butter in a 9-inch square baking pan in the preheating oven. Spread it over the bottom and sides of the pan.

In a mixing bowl, combine the dry ingredients. In another bowl, mix together the egg and buttermilk and stir them into the dry ingredients. Pour the mixture into the hot, buttered pan and bake for 25 minutes, or until it tests done. Serve warm with melted butter.

Makes nine 3-inch servings

Soufflé
Spoon Bread

ॐ

Spoon breads are more like soufflés or puddings, but they really are breads that you can scoop onto your plate with a spoon. Serve this one with sausages, fruit, or barbecued poultry or pork.

2 cups water	4 eggs, separated
1 cup yellow stone-ground cornmeal	½ cup milk
	½ cup all-purpose flour
1 tablespoon butter	2 teaspoons baking powder
1 teaspoon salt	2 tablespoons sugar

Preheat the oven to 400° F. Grease a 2-quart soufflé dish.

In a medium saucepan, bring the water to a boil. Whisk in the cornmeal, then add the butter and salt and cook 5 minutes until thickened, stirring until smooth. Remove from the heat and let cool. Stir the egg yolks and milk together, and add to the cornmeal. Mix the flour, baking powder, and sugar and beat into the cornmeal mixture. Beat the egg whites until stiff and fold into the cornmeal mixture. Pour into the prepared baking dish and bake for 30 to 35 minutes, or until set. Serve immediately.

Makes 6 servings

Cheese-Topped Corn Bread

☙

There are as many versions of corn bread as there are cooks, I suppose. This one makes a fine main dish topped with creamed chicken or just a simple cheese sauce.

4 slices bacon, cut into
½-inch dice

¼ cup minced scallions,
including tops

2 jalapeño peppers, seeded
and chopped

1 cup yellow stone-ground
cornmeal

1 cup all-purpose flour

2½ teaspoons baking powder

½ teaspoon baking soda

½ teaspoon salt

1 egg

¾ cup plain low-fat yogurt

¾ cup milk

4 tablespoons (½ stick)
butter, melted

½ cup shredded Monterey
Jack cheese

Preheat the oven to 400° F. In a heavy skillet, cook the bacon over medium heat until crisp, then drain, reserving 2 tablespoons of the drippings. Spread the reserved drippings into a 9-inch square baking pan or a 9-inch heavy cast-iron skillet.

In a large mixing bowl, combine the bacon, scallions, and peppers. In another bowl, combine the cornmeal, flour, baking powder, soda, and salt, and add to the bacon mixture. Mix well.

Make a well in the center of the ingredients and add the egg, yogurt, milk, and melted butter. Stir them together, then mix just until the dry ingredients are moistened. Pour into the prepared pan or skillet and sprinkle with the cheese. Bake for 20 to 25 minutes, or until it tests done. Cut into wedges or squares and serve hot.

Makes nine 3-inch servings or 8 wedges

Hot Pepper and
Bacon Corn Bread

⤶

This hearty, colorful loaf is almost a main dish in itself. I make it in a cast-iron skillet and cut it into thick wedges to serve with a mixed green salad for brunch or lunch. Even though there are three peppers in the bread, it isn't fiery, just pleasantly hot. But please wear rubber gloves when you seed and chop the peppers!

1 strip bacon, cut into
  ½-inch dice
1 cup yellow stone-ground
  cornmeal
1 cup canned cream-style
  corn
1 cup (4 ounces) shredded
  Monterey Jack or farmer
  cheese

½ cup corn oil
½ cup buttermilk
1 teaspoon baking soda
½ teaspoon salt
2 eggs
3 jalapeño peppers, seeded
  and chopped

Preheat the oven to 400° F. Distribute the bacon pieces in the bottom of a 12-inch nonstick cast-iron skillet and place into the oven as it preheats until the bacon pieces are crisp. Spread the drippings and bacon around the pan to coat it evenly.

Meanwhile, stir all of the remaining ingredients together in a bowl until blended. Spoon the cornmeal mixture into the hot skillet so that it is evenly distributed. Return to the oven and bake for 20 minutes, or until browned and crusty. Serve hot, cut in wedges.

Makes one 12-inch round loaf, 6—8 servings

Yankee
Corn Bread

✦

As a Northerner, I grew up preferring corn bread that wasn't quite as dry and crumbly as the classic Southern variety. This bread has the texture of cornmeal but the lightness that a high percentage of wheat flour adds to the mixture.

1½ cups all-purpose flour
1 tablespoon baking powder
½ teaspoon salt
½ cup yellow stone-ground cornmeal

¼ cup sugar
2 eggs, beaten
1 cup milk
3 tablespoons butter, melted

Preheat the oven to 425° F. Generously butter an 8- or 9-inch square baking pan.

In a large bowl, stir the flour, baking powder, salt, cornmeal, and sugar together until well blended. In a small bowl, blend the eggs, milk, and butter. Add to the dry ingredients, stirring only until they are moistened. Pour into the prepared baking pan and bake for 25 to 30 minutes, or until golden on top. Serve warm, cut into squares, split, and buttered.

Makes nine 3-inch servings

Cracklin'
Corn Bread

ॐ

Real "cracklings" are crispy
bits left after most of the fat has been rendered by cook-
ing pork, usually side pork. In this recipe, I've used
crisp cooked bacon—I love the smoky taste it adds.

½ pound bacon
1 cup yellow or white stone-
    ground cornmeal
1 cup all-purpose flour
⅓ cup sugar
2½ teaspoons baking powder

¼ teaspoon salt
1 cup buttermilk
6 tablespoons (¾ stick)
    butter, melted
1 egg

Preheat the oven to 425° F. Grease a 9-inch square pan.

Cook the bacon until crisp. Drain it well, then crumble it into
a mixing bowl. Add all of the remaining ingredients in order,
then stir until blended.

Pour the mixture into the prepared pan. Bake for 20 to 25
minutes, or until the edges are lightly browned. Cut into squares
while warm and serve with butter.

Makes nine 3-inch servings

OLD-FASHIONED COFFEE CAKES

৯৯

Blueberry Gingerbread

Streusel Raspberry Coffee Cake

Walnut Pear Coffee Cake

Apple Pie Coffee Cake

Sour Cream Cinnamon Coffee Cake

Quick Sally Lunn

Whole-Wheat Coffee Cake

Blueberry Gingerbread

❧

Not just for breakfast—this makes a delightful old-fashioned dessert when topped with softly whipped cream.

½ cup vegetable oil	2 cups all-purpose flour
1 cup plus 2 tablespoons sugar	1 teaspoon baking soda
	1 teaspoon ground cinnamon
1 egg	½ teaspoon ground ginger
½ cup light molasses	½ teaspoon ground nutmeg
1 cup fresh (or frozen, thawed) blueberries	½ teaspoon salt
	1 cup buttermilk

Preheat the oven to 350° F. Grease a 9-inch square cake pan.

In a large mixing bowl, beat the oil, sugar, and egg until light. Add the molasses and beat until thick. In a small bowl, toss the blueberries with 2 tablespoons of the flour until well coated. Mix the remaining flour with the dry ingredients. Add the flour mixture and the buttermilk alternately to the creamed mixture, and blend until smooth. Fold in the blueberries. Turn into the prepared pan. Bake for 45 to 50 minutes, or until it tests done. Serve warm.

Makes one 9-inch square cake

Streusel Raspberry Coffee Cake

ॐ

This is a delicate, buttery cake with raspberries and a crunchy streusel topping.

1½ cups all-purpose flour

½ cup granulated sugar

2 teaspoons baking powder

1 egg

½ cup (1 stick) butter, melted

½ cup milk

1 cup fresh or frozen, whole
   unsweetened raspberries

STREUSEL TOPPING

¼ cup chopped pecans

¼ cup brown sugar, packed

¼ cup all-purpose flour

2 tablespoons butter, melted

Preheat the oven to 375° F. Butter a 9-inch square cake pan.

In a large bowl, stir together the flour, granulated sugar, and baking powder. In a small bowl, mix the egg, butter, and milk. Stir the liquids into the dry ingredients just until blended. Spoon half the mixture into the prepared pan. Top with the raspberries and then spoon the remaining dough over them.

In another bowl, combine the pecans, brown sugar, and flour. Stir in the melted butter until the mixture resembles moist crumbs. Sprinkle it over the top of the dough in the pan.

Bake for 25 to 30 minutes, or until the topping is golden.

Makes one 9-inch square cake

Walnut Pear Coffee Cake

❧

Chunks of pear are moist bits atop a sour-cream coffee cake. The top is crisp with a crumbly brown sugar and nut layer.

¼ cup (½ stick) butter, at room temperature

½ cup granulated sugar

½ teaspoon vanilla extract

1 egg

1 cup all-purpose flour

½ teaspoon baking powder

½ teaspoon baking soda

¼ teaspoon salt

½ cup sour cream

1 large ripe Bosc or red Bartlett pear, peeled and cut into ½-inch dice

CRISP TOPPING

¼ cup brown sugar, packed

¼ cup all-purpose flour

1 teaspoon ground cinnamon

2 tablespoons (¼ stick) butter, softened

½ cup chopped walnuts

Preheat the oven to 350° F. Butter a 9-inch springform or square baking pan.

Cream the butter and granulated sugar until blended; beat in the vanilla and egg until light. Stir the flour, baking powder, soda, and salt together and add to the creamed mixture along with the sour cream, blending well. Spread the batter in the prepared pan and sprinkle the pears over evenly and press them into the batter slightly.

Mix the topping ingredients until blended and crumbly, and sprinkle over the pears.

Bake for 45 to 50 minutes, or until the top is browned and it tests done. Cool and cut into squares.

Makes one 9-inch round or square cake

Apple Pie Coffee Cake

❧

Topped with sautéed apple slices, this cake is heavenly with morning coffee or even for dessert, served with a pouf of whipped cream.

1 ¼ cups all-purpose flour
½ cup sugar
1 teaspoon baking powder
¼ teaspoon baking soda
¼ teaspoon salt
1 teaspoon cinnamon

½ cup (1 stick) butter, at room temperature
½ cup milk
1 egg
1 teaspoon vanilla extract

TOPPING

½ cup all-purpose flour
½ cup plus 2 tablespoons sugar
3 tablespoons butter

2 cups sliced tart apple (2 medium, peeled and cored)
1 ½ teaspoons ground cinnamon
¼ teaspoon ground nutmeg

Preheat the oven to 350° F. Grease and flour a 9-inch springform pan or square baking pan.

Blend the flour, sugar, baking powder, soda, salt, and cinnamon together in a large bowl. With an electric mixer, blend in the butter until the mixture is crumbly. In another bowl, mix the milk, egg, and vanilla until blended and stir into the flour mixture until the batter is well mixed. Turn into the prepared baking pan and spread evenly.

For the topping, combine the flour, ½ cup of the sugar, and 2 tablespoons of the butter until the mixture looks like coarse crumbs. Sprinkle half of the mixture over the batter in the pan.

In a heavy skillet, melt the remaining 1 tablespoon of butter and add the apple slices; sauté for 2 to 3 minutes on high heat, just until the apples are cooked, stirring constantly. Sprinkle the 2 tablespoons of sugar over them and add the cinnamon and nutmeg. Spread the mixture over the crumbs in the pan. Top with the remaining crumbs. Bake for 1 hour, or until the top is golden brown. Remove from the oven and cool for 10 minutes. If using a springform pan, loosen the cake by running a knife around the inside edge of the pan. Remove the ring and finish cooling on a rack with the bottom of the pan still in place.

Makes one 9-inch springform or square cake

Sour Cream Cinnamon Coffee Cake

❧

Bake this coffee cake in a fancy tube pan such as a bundt pan or kugelhof pan. The cinnamon-and-nut layer running through the center and covering the top of the cake makes it extra special.

1 cup (2 sticks) butter, at
   room temperature
1 cup sugar
2 eggs
1 cup sour cream, stirred

2 cups all-purpose flour
1 ½ teaspoons baking powder
½ teaspoon baking soda
1 teaspoon vanilla extract

FILLING AND TOPPING

¾ cup finely chopped walnuts
   or pecans

1 teaspoon ground cinnamon
2 tablespoons sugar

Preheat the oven to 350° F. Butter and flour a 9- or 10-inch fancy tube pan or bundt cake pan.

In a large mixing bowl, beat the butter, sugar, and eggs together until light. Blend in the sour cream. In another bowl, mix the flour, baking powder, and soda together and add to the creamed mixture, beating until blended. Add the vanilla. Spoon half the batter into the prepared pan.

For the filling and topping, mix the nuts, cinnamon, and sugar until blended. Sprinkle half the mixture over the batter in the pan. Top with the remaining batter and then the remainder of the nut mixture.

Bake for 45 to 55 minutes, or until it tests done. Let cool for 10 minutes, then remove from the pan.

Makes one 10-inch bundt cake

Quick
Sally Lunn

୬

This yeast-risen coffee cake probably originated in Bath, England, where a woman named Sally Lunn sold tea cakes in the 18th century. This quick version is leavened with baking powder instead of yeast.

½ cup (1 stick) butter, at room temperature

⅓ cup sugar

3 eggs, at room temperature

2 cups all-purpose flour

3 teaspoons baking powder

½ teaspoon salt

1 cup milk, at room temperature

Preheat the oven to 425° F. Lightly grease a 10-inch tube pan.

In a large bowl, cream the butter with the sugar until blended. Beat in the eggs until light.

In another bowl, stir together the flour, baking powder, and salt. Add half the dry ingredients to the creamed ingredients alternately with half the milk, then repeat. Stir until the ingredients are just blended. Turn into the prepared pan and bake for 45 to 50 minutes, or until it tests done. Serve while still hot, separating the cake into thick wedges with two forks.

Makes one 10-inch tube bread

Whole-Wheat Coffee Cake

꙳

Light, not too sweet, and grainy, this coffee cake is best served warm. However, you can bake it and freeze it if you wish.

1 egg

½ cup granulated sugar

½ cup milk

3 tablespoons butter, melted

1½ cups whole-wheat flour

1½ teaspoons baking powder

½ teaspoon salt

TOPPING

½ cup brown sugar, packed

¼ cup whole-wheat flour

¼ cup finely chopped walnuts

3 tablespoons butter, softened

1 teaspoon ground cinnamon

Preheat the oven to 375° F. Grease an 8-inch square cake pan.

In a mixing bowl, beat the egg with the granulated sugar, milk, and butter until light. Stir in the flour, baking powder, and salt, blending well. Turn the mixture into the cake pan.

Stir the topping ingredients until the mixture is crumbly. Sprinkle the crumbs over the top of the cake. Bake for 20 to 25 minutes, or until it tests done and the crumbs are golden brown.

Makes one 8-inch square cake

HOLIDAY AND ETHNIC CAKES

Quick Kugelhof

Saffron Kage

Scandinavian Quick Julekage

Stollen

Quick Panettone

Quick Kugelhof

❧

Kugelhof is a classic holiday bread with Germanic-Alsatian roots. Baked in a special fluted tube pan, traditional kugelhof is yeast-raised; this is a quick—but still delicious—version.

1 cup (2 sticks) butter

1 cup granulated sugar

5 eggs

3½ cups all-purpose flour

3 teaspoons baking powder

½ teaspoon salt

1 cup milk

1 cup golden raisins

1 teaspoon grated lemon rind

1 teaspoon vanilla extract

    Powdered sugar

Preheat the oven to 350° F. Grease and flour a 10-inch fancy tube pan.

In a large bowl, cream the butter and sugar. Add the eggs and beat until light. In another bowl, stir together the flour, baking powder, and salt. Add this mixture and the milk to the creamed mixture to make a smooth batter. Add the raisins, lemon rind, and vanilla. Turn into the prepared pan. Bake for 45 to 50 minutes, or until it tests done. Cool in the pan 10 minutes, then invert onto a rack. Dust with powdered sugar.

Makes one 10-inch tube cake

Saffron Kage

※

Saffron-flavored breads are traditional Swedish holiday breads. Often yeast-raised, this quick version is popular with many folks.

1 cup (2 sticks) butter	1 cup milk
1 cup granulated sugar	1/8 teaspoon saffron
5 eggs	1 cup golden raisins
3 1/2 cups all-purpose flour	1 teaspoon vanilla extract
3 teaspoons baking powder	Powdered sugar
1/2 teaspoon salt	

Preheat the oven to 350° F. Grease and flour a 9-inch or 10-inch fancy tube pan.

In a large bowl, cream the butter and granulated sugar. Beat in the eggs until the mixture is light. In another bowl, stir the flour, baking powder, and salt together. Mix the milk and saffron together and add to the creamed mixture along with the dry ingredients. Stir until smooth. Add the raisins and vanilla. Turn into the prepared pan. Bake for 45 to 50 minutes, or until it tests done. Cool in the pan for 10 minutes, then invert onto a rack. Dust with powdered sugar.

Makes one 9-inch or 10-inch tube cake

Scandinavian
Quick Julekage

❧

Julekage is traditionally a yeast-risen bread that is served with cookies and coffee during the Christmas season in Scandinavia. Rich and light, it is flavored with cardamom and almonds and usually is iced and decorated with raisins or fruits.

1 whole egg plus 2 egg yolks

½ cup granulated sugar

½ cup (1 stick) butter, melted and cooled

1 teaspoon crushed cardamom seeds

½ cup slivered almonds

½ cup chopped mixed candied fruits

3 cups all-purpose flour

2 teaspoons baking powder

½ teaspoon salt

1 cup milk

GLAZE AND DECORATION

¼ cup powdered sugar

1–2 teaspoons hot, strong coffee

Raisins, whole almonds, candied cherries

Preheat the oven to 325° F. Grease and flour a 9-inch round cake pan.

In a large bowl, beat the egg, yolks, and granulated sugar together until thick and pale yellow. Beat in the melted butter, then add the cardamom, almonds, and fruits. In another bowl, mix the flour, baking powder, and salt, and add half to the creamed mixture, then stir in half the milk. Add the remaining flour and milk and blend well. Turn the mixture into the prepared pan, shaping the top so that the center is higher than the edges. Bake for about 1 ½ hours, or until it tests done. Remove from the pan and cool on a rack.

Before serving, mix the powdered sugar with enough hot, strong coffee to make a glaze. Brush or drizzle it over the cooled loaf. Decorate with raisins, almonds, and cherries.

Makes one 9-inch round loaf

Stollen

❧

Stollen is Germany's traditional Christmas bread, laden with fruits and nuts and topped with a generous coating of powdered sugar. Traditional stollen is yeast-raised, but this new version is just as delicious!

2½ cups all-purpose flour

2 teaspoons baking powder

¾ cup granulated sugar

½ teaspoon salt

½ teaspoon freshly ground
   nutmeg

¼ teaspoon freshly ground
   cardamom seeds

1 cup blanched almonds,
   pulverized in a food
   processor

½ cup (1 stick) butter

1 cup ricotta cheese

1 egg

½ teaspoon vanilla extract

¼ teaspoon almond extract

2 tablespoons dark rum

½ cup dried currants

½ cup golden raisins

¼ cup chopped candied lemon
   or orange peel

3 tablespoons butter, melted

2 tablespoons powdered sugar

Preheat the oven to 350° F. Grease and flour a baking sheet.

In a large bowl, or in the work bowl of a food processor with the steel blade in place, combine the flour, baking powder, granulated sugar, salt, nutmeg, cardamom, and almonds. Slice the butter into the mixture and cut into the flour with a fork or pastry blender, or pulse the food processor, until the mixture resembles coarse crumbs. (If using the food processor, turn the mixture out into a large bowl at this point.)

In a small bowl, blend the ricotta, egg, vanilla, almond extract, rum, currants, raisins, and lemon peel. Stir this mixture into the flour mixture until all the ingredients are moistened. Shape the dough into a ball and turn it out onto a lightly floured board. Knead it lightly, about 10 turns, until the dough is smooth.

Roll the dough out on a floured board to form an oval about 8 x 10 inches. With a rolling pin, crease the dough just off center, along the length of the oval. Brush with 1 tablespoon of the melted butter. Fold the smaller section over the larger one. Place on the prepared baking sheet and bake for about 45 minutes, or until the crust is browned and it tests done.

Brush with the remaining butter and sprinkle with the powdered sugar. Serve warm. You may wrap the bread and allow it to mellow for 2 to 3 days; or freeze it, if you wish.

Makes one 12-inch loaf, 16 servings

Quick Panettone

ℨ

Panettone is a light and cakelike bread that is flavored with anise, pine nuts, and grated lemon peel. On a holiday eve, serve it with a sweet wine or with espresso or cappucino. Traditionally, panettone is made with yeast and baked in a high, round metal mold, but a pan collared with wax paper or parchment makes a fine substitute.

2 eggs

½ cup sugar

½ cup (1 stick) butter, melted and cooled

1 teaspoon grated lemon peel

1 teaspoon crushed anise seed

¼ cup pine nuts or slivered almonds

¼ cup golden raisins

¼ cup mixed candied fruits, chopped

1 teaspoon anise extract

1 teaspoon lemon extract

3 cups all-purpose flour

2 teaspoons baking powder

½ teaspoon salt

1 cup milk

Preheat the oven to 325° F. Grease a panettone mold. If using an 8-inch round cake pan, grease it well, and cut a 3-inch-wide strip of brown paper, parchment, or wax paper long enough to go all around the rim of the pan. Fit the paper onto the *inside* edge of the pan (the grease will help make it stand up and stay in place) to make a tall collar.

In a large bowl, beat the eggs and sugar until thick and pale yellow. Beat in the melted butter, lemon peel, anise seed, nuts, raisins, fruits, and anise and lemon extracts. In a small bowl, mix the flour, baking powder, and salt and blend into the creamed mixture alternately with the milk. Turn the mixture into the prepared baking pan. Bake for 1 hour and 45 minutes, or until the bread is well browned and tests done. Cool the bread in the pan for 10 minutes, then turn it out onto a rack to finish cooling. To serve, remove the paper and cut the bread into wedges.

Makes one 8-inch loaf

SPREADS FOR BREADS

৯৯

Herbed Chèvre Spread

Savory Herbed Cheese

Spiced Honey

Orange Cream Cheese Spread

Apricot Cream Cheese Spread

Whipped Spiced Amaretto Butter

Herbed
Chèvre Spread

❦

This spread is great on savory loaves of Soda Bread (page 64), Caraway Beer Bread (page 65), or Australian Damper (page 68). Try it instead of mayonnaise on ham sandwiches.

½ cup (1 stick) butter, at room temperature
1 (5-ounce) package Chèvre cheese, at room temperature

¼ cup minced parsley
1 tablespoon minced fresh tarragon or 1 teaspoon dried

In a deep mixer bowl, with an electric hand mixer, beat the butter until fluffy; beat in the cheese until the mixture is well blended. Stir in the parsley and tarragon. Serve immediately or cover and refrigerate. Allow the chilled spread to come to room temperature before serving.

Makes about 1½ cups

Savory
Herbed Cheese

✺

You can make this cheese ahead and freeze it. Bring it to room temperature for easier spreading over any sliced savory bread.

1 (8-ounce) package cream cheese, at room temperature

1 cup (2 sticks) butter, at room temperature

1 garlic clove, minced or pressed

2 tablespoons finely chopped fresh herbs (e. g., parsley, chervil, tarragon, thyme, and rosemary)

3 tablespoons fresh lemon juice

In a deep mixer bowl, with an electric hand mixer, or in the food processor with the steel blade in place, combine the cream cheese and butter. Beat or process until light and fluffy. Add the garlic, the herbs (alone or in combination), and lemon juice and beat until blended. Turn the mixture into a 16-ounce (2-cup) serving crock or bowl. Cover and refrigerate 2 to 4 hours for the flavors to blend. Remove from the refrigerator about 1 hour ahead of time to serve at room temperature.

Makes 2 cups

Spiced Honey

⤷

This makes a wonderful gift tucked into a basket with freshly baked Kugelhof (page 104). Spiced Honey is also wonderful with Irish Soda Bread (page 64), made with or without the herbs.

It is easy to make Spiced Honey in any amount, as the recipe is quite flexible. It should be made at least 6 days in advance for the honey to pick up the flavors of the spices. The longer you keep it, the more pronounced the flavors become. If the honey gets too spicy, dilute it with a fresh supply.

*1 cup mild honey (such as
    clover honey)*
*1-inch piece crystallized
    ginger*

4 or 5 whole cloves
1 cinnamon stick
2-inch strip of lemon zest

Fill an 8-ounce jar with honey. Stud the ginger with the whole cloves and press into the honey. Add the cinnamon stick and lemon zest. Cover and keep at room temperature for about 6 days to develop the flavor.

Makes 1 cup

Orange Cream Cheese Spread

࿇

Make this the day before you plan to serve it with fruit-nut, tea, or brown breads. Serve it at room temperature for spreadability.

1 (8-ounce) package cream cheese, softened

1 tablespoon orange-flavored liqueur

1 tablespoon freshly grated orange rind

In a deep mixer bowl, with an electric hand mixer, whip the cream cheese until fluffy. Slowly add the orange liqueur and grated orange rind, beating until blended. Refrigerate to store, but bring to room temperature before serving.

Makes 1 cup

Apricot Cream Cheese Spread

෴

This is heavenly on warm slices of fruit-nut bread. Refrigerated in a covered jar, it will keep for up to a week.

1 (3-ounce) package cream
   cheese, at room temperature
¼ cup apricot jam

1 teaspoon grated lemon zest
1 tablespoon freshly squeezed
   lemon juice

In a small, deep mixer bowl, with an electric hand mixer, whip the cream cheese until light and fluffy. Beat in the apricot jam, lemon zest, and lemon juice.

Makes ¾ cup

Whipped Spiced Amaretto Butter

১৯

Serve this flavorful butter with any holiday bread or with warm, sliced tea bread.

½ cup (1 stick) unsalted butter

2 tablespoons warm water

2 tablespoons Amaretto or almond-flavored liqueur

1 teaspoon freshly ground cardamom or ½ teaspoon freshly grated nutmeg

In a deep mixer bowl, with an electric hand mixer, whip the butter until fluffy, adding the warm water very gradually. Slowly beat in the Amaretto. Blend in the cardamom or nutmeg. Turn the mixture into a serving bowl and chill just long enough to firm the butter, but not so long that it is hard, or it will crumble rather than spread on the bread.

Makes about ⅔ cup

INDEX